POINTS OF THE

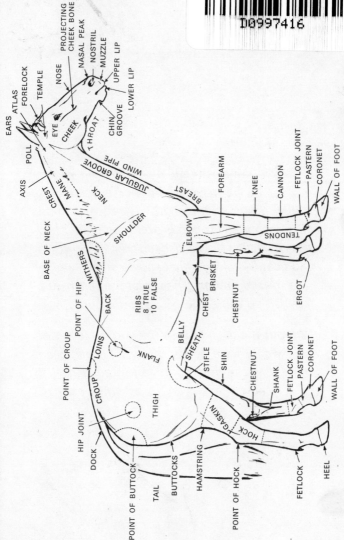

A Ladybird Book
Series 682

*Before the steam engine and the motor car
were invented, the horse was man's
chief means of transport. It carried him on
its back, transported his goods over rough mountain
passes, pulled his carriages and carts in town
and country, plodded patiently across acres of
farm-land dragging heavy farm implements,
rounded up cattle and carried armies into war.*

*Without the useful horse the whole history of
the world would have been different. It has been
more than the friend of man for thousands of
years —it has been his essential partner.*

A Ladybird book about
HORSES

by NANCY SCOTT
with illustrations by B. H. ROBINSON

Publishers Wills & Hepworth Ltd Loughborough
First published 1968   ©   *Printed in England*

The Horse Family

Ponies, donkeys, wild asses, zebras and mules are members of the Horse family, the EQUIDAE. Ponies are small horses below 14.2 hands in height. The height of a horse is taken from the highest part of the withers, the shoulders, down to the ground. It is given in 'hands' and inches; a 'hand' measuring four inches.

Donkeys are domesticated wild asses. Zebras are striped black and white, and mules are the off-spring of a horse and a donkey.

All the members of this family Equidae have horny hoofs, teeth specially adapted for grazing on grass, and long tails of whiplike hair which are used to flick away irritating and harmful types of flies.

Horses can live long lives, the longest so far recorded being fifty years. To horsemen the word 'horse' means a male. The female horse is called a mare. A young mare is a filly, and a young male a colt. A full grown male is a stallion.

The mare gives birth to her foal eleven months after mating. The foal is born with its eyes open, and is able to stand unsupported a few minutes after birth. To see the dainty, little foal rise totteringly to its feet, and take its first few, hesitant steps, is a breathtaking sight and one which man has watched in wonder since earliest times.

7214 0114 7

A mare and foal

Dawn Horse

It is hard to believe that the little animal in the illustration, less than a foot in height, is the ancestor of the horses we know. Yet scientists say that it is, and that HYRACOTHERIUM lived some sixty million years ago in the Eocene period of time.

The word Eocene means 'dawn of the new', and this period lasted about thirty to thirty-five million years. It was the first major period of the Age of Mammals, and during that time the earth was populated with strange, primitive animals, many of them thickset, heavily built creatures with short legs. Among them was Hyracotherium, more popularly known as Eohippus which means in Greek—the 'Dawn Horse'.

Dawn Horse had neither horns nor claws with which to protect itself, so it depended on speed to escape from its enemies. At first this small animal had four toes on its front feet, and three toes on the hind feet. But over the years a great change came about in the formation of these feet. The centre toe, which bore most of the animal's weight when running, grew larger, while the outer toes became smaller until they disappeared almost entirely, leaving the one large central toe on each foot, now known as the hoof.

Eohippus—the Dawn Horse and (below) the evolution of the horse's foot

Cave-man's horses

Dawn Horse passed through many stages of evolution until the day when man inhabited the earth. By that time it had become a large animal, bigger than the modern donkey, with heavy limbs, a large rough head and a wild, bristly mane.

Fortunately we do not have to rely only on a few bones dug out of the earth to picture in our minds this early wild horse. Early cave-man drew this animal on the walls of the caves in which he lived many thousands of years ago, and these drawings may still be seen to-day. They show us vividly how coarse, strong and altogether wild-looking were those ancestors of our elegant race-horses, stocky donkeys, sturdy mountain and moorland ponies and dainty little Shetland ponies.

No-one can tell when or how the wild horse became tame enough for man to use for transporting himself and his goods. But for thousands and thousands of years, until the steam-engine was invented in the 19th century, the horse was the most important means of land transport all over the world.

At first, early man hunted the wild horse for food, just as he hunted all wild animals; but one day he discovered that the horse could be used in a better way—to carry him long distances, quickly and easily, and to give him greater speed in hunting elusive and swift-footed animals. Later he used the horse to drag sledges on which could be piled the spoils of his hunt, or the logs he needed for building his home and for his fires.

A cave-painter at work

Original wild stock

From the early cave-man's drawings, and from later rock carvings, sculptures, pictures, coins of historic times and some skeletal remains, we can trace the story of the original, wild horse stock of the world. Scientists divide this into roughly three groups based on geographical situation: the northern, cold-blooded type, the southern, hot-blooded type, and the mixed, warm-blooded type which has developed by the mixing and inter-breeding of northern and southern breeds.

The northern, cold-blooded type (Equus Caballus Frigidus) and its descendants were all powerful, heavy-boned animals which could stand up to very cold weather. Their skin was thick, hair coarse, eyes angular, narrow and set high in the skull near the coarse, blunted ears. All had short necks. They were the ancestors of the horses known generally as the Great Horses of Europe—the cart-horses (with some mixture of oriental blood in later years), the large horses of ancient China and Persia, the Mongolian and Germanic breeds, and some of the heavily-built European ponies.

Among these northern types is the ancient Wild Horse, now known as Equus Przevalskii and named after the Russian explorer, Colonel N. M. Przevalski, who first brought news of this existing wild breed to zoologists. For thousands of years this horse has lived wild in the remote parts of Mongolia, Russia and the borders of China. It is the only true wild horse left in the world to-day. There are many breeds of horses roaming wild in different parts of the world, but all are descendants of domestic horses that have escaped from captivity.

The true wild horse

Southern stock

The original southern, hot-blooded stock was Arabian. It was a much slimmer and finer breed of horse, with large, round, flashing eyes set low in the head, sharply cut ears and a long, arched neck. A horse of true Arabian stock has its tail set high, and holds it high, too. It is a much livelier animal than the northern type, and it is from this type that the fastest racing stocks have developed.

In ancient Arabia, the pedigree of the Arab horse can be traced back some five thousand years: a wild mare was captured by Baz the great-great-grandson of Noah, and he named her Baz. This is believed to be the first authentic record we have of a wild horse being captured. These wild horses were roaming in the ancient land of Arabia when it was 'a land of trees and rivers' and not the arid desert region which most of it is to-day.

The Arab people were then nomads, just as many of them still are to-day. Nomads have no fixed home, but journey from place to place wherever the best pasture-land and water can be found.

The ancient Arabs worshipped the sun, moon and stars and a horse-idol called Ya'uk. In Southern Arabia the idol was called Ya'bub, meaning 'a swift horse'. On the walls of some ancient Egyptian temples can be seen carvings of these pure Arab type horses. These horses were brought into Egypt by the Arab invaders in time of war, about 2500–1500 B.C.

Horses of the original Arabian stock

The horse in war

The Great Horse of Europe is the ancestor of all the heavy breeds of horses used in war, and for agriculture and haulage work.

In A.D. 378 the Goths defeated the Romans at Adrianople, and historians tell us that this must be regarded as the first great victory of heavy cavalry (soldiers on horseback) over the heavy infantry (soldiers on foot). From then on, and for many hundreds of years, soldiers fought from horseback as well as from the ground.

From the middle of the sixth century, armour was used for protection, and by A.D. 1300 men were equipping themselves from top to toe in plate armour. By that time the Great Horse had reached the size and strength needed to carry the great weight of rider and armour.

In A.D. 1200, King John brought into this country, from Europe, a hundred dray stallions to blend with English stock and so increase its size and strength. In 1377 Richard II imported even larger numbers of these great battle horses.

The battles between armies of armour-clad men mounted on these massive horses were very terrible indeed. An injured horse became a mad raging beast, plunging, rearing, and stampeding, and if a man fell from his horse he stood little chance of survival. There were very few wounded soldiers carried off the field alive in those days.

*Armour-clad men and
armour-clad horses*

Breeding the heavy, weight-carrying horses

The breeding of the heavy horse reached its peak in the reign of Henry VIII (1509–1547). The King was a heavy man, and it is said that he frequently tired out eight to ten horses during a day's hunting. But not only did he himself need a great many big horses in his stables, but more and more heavy horses were needed at that time to carry his armoured soldiers. So laws were passed compelling every horse-breeder to concentrate mainly on the heavy, weight-carrying horses and much less on the lighter breeds. To help this scheme along, many fine horses were imported from Holland, Germany and Italy.

Our mountain and moorland ponies escaped this breeding-out of the smaller, lighter horses, as they could not so easily be caught on the wild hillsides and open moorlands.

The laws were very strict regarding horses in those days. The richer a man, the more horses he was expected to keep. The reason was that in time of war a nobleman or man of wealth was expected to provide a given number of horses to take part in the battles.

In addition to the horses kept by the rich, there were farms for breeding cavalry Great Horses. Large herds of horses could then be seen in the fields, just as we see herds of cattle and flocks of sheep in our fields to-day.

A medieval horse farm

Lighter armour becomes essential

The heavier the breed of horse, the less its speed; and when armour became thicker and heavier, to withstand bullets instead of arrows, then the speed of the horse became even less.

By the end of the 16th century the Great Horses were still bearing armoured men into battle, men whose armour was even heavier. They were the cuirassiers, horse-soldiers clad in thick, heavy, shot-proof iron armour which was fastened over the breast and back with straps and buckles.

Eventually this extra-heavy armour slowed down the speed of the Great Horse to an impracticable pace—impracticable because there were many occasions in battle when speed was essential. Frequently the enemy escaped simply because they were mounted on lighter horses of the southern breeds, and were not clad in such weighty armour, looking like 'regiments of lobsters'—as the cuirassiers were often mockingly called.

When Oliver Cromwell formed his New Model Army in 1645 the soldiers were no longer clothed in massive armour, so the name cuirassier went out of use in the English army. Instead the new, lighter cavalry were called harquebusiers and dragoons. A harquebusier, or arquebuse as it was sometimes called, was the name of the type of hand-gun they carried. A dragoon was a mounted infantryman and carried a 'fire-spitting musket'.

*Dragoons of Cromwell's
New Model Army*

The horse in transport

For centuries, certain breeds of the heavy horse were specially kept for riding, and these became famous for the 'ambling pace' which was very gentle and comfortable for travelling. Horse-drawn carts and wagons were used for carrying goods and for work on the farms. There were also carriages called by various names—chares, cars, chariots, caroches and whirlicotes—especially designed to carry passengers. In Britain it was the height of luxury to own one of these, and only the richest in the land possessed such a vehicle. The early carriages were rarely used as they were shockingly uncomfortable to ride in, because springs were not invented until 1690, and consequently they jerked, bounded, bumped and crashed along roads which in those days were full of big pot-holes and ruts. One can easily imagine how painful such journeys must have been.

Some of the early carriages became 'family heirlooms', their cost and history being carefully recorded in family documents. One carriage, built in the year 1363 for a certain Lady Eleanor, cost one thousand pounds, which was then the equivalent in value of one thousand, six hundred oxen.

Another way in which some people travelled was by ornamented horse-litter. This vehicle was like a sedan chair supported on poles and carried by shaft-horses before and behind. So long as the horses ambled in step, this ride must have been reasonably comfortable, but what happened when the horses broke step, or a shaft broke, is best left to one's imagination.

Various forms of horse transport

Carrying the mail

The horse was also used to carry letters from town to town. For many years the post-rider's uniform was as colourful as the early 19th century one shown in our illustration. Some were even more elaborate: the 16th century post-rider, who carried the mails from London to Edinburgh, sported fur tops to his boots which were called 'spatterdashes', and his hat was shaped like an earl's coronet.

In the 16th century, that journey took seven days, and the post-rider was expected to blow his horn three times in every mile, also whenever he met anything on the road or passed through a town. Horses were changed frequently, at ten mile stages, and each postmaster was ordered to keep four horses and two horns ready. Also he was given the right to commandeer other people's horses for the mail-service if necessary.

The post-riders were not allowed to pack more than thirty pounds weight of mail onto their horses, or to ride faster than seven miles an hour in summer and six in winter. The charge for mail delivered in this way was twopence or twopence halfpenny per mile. This was raised to threepence per mile in 1609.

But the supervision of the service was difficult over such a long journey. All too often horses were over-ridden and killed, or they were stolen sometimes direct from the rider or from the stables. Frequently the post-riders were bribed to carry more weight than they should. In fact the life of a post-horse was certainly not a happy one, nor a long one in many cases.

A post-horse and rider

General transport during the 17th century and after

Horse-drawn coaches for hire were started in London in the early 17th century. These were called Hackney coaches. Many of these coaches were drawn by horses of the Shire breed who were descended from the old 'English War Horse', the Great Horse.

By 1636, there were six thousand horse-drawn Hackney coaches rattling through the streets of London, which was a much smaller city than it is to-day. The citizens of London called them Hackney Hell Carts, and protested loudly about them. They blocked the narrow streets in a dangerous way and one person wrote that 'the earth trembled and shook and the casements went shatter-tatter from the tumbling din'.

There were horse-drawn coaches on the country roads, too, travelling from London to other towns, and back.

In the 17th, 18th and 19th centuries the streets of London, and other big cities, were packed with horse-drawn vehicles of all kinds as well as people riding on horseback. There were private carriages, hackney, mail and passenger coaches, large horse-buses (19th century), carts carrying goods for sale, carts delivering and collecting goods to and from markets, warehouses and docks, in fact horse-drawn vehicles were used for transporting everything for which we now use motor vehicles and trains. The noise in the city streets must have been indescribable. Many of the roads were stone cobbled, and as neither pneumatic nor rubber tyres had yet been invented, the clatter and rattle must certainly have been just as the 17th century writer described it—'a tumbling din'.

London in the late 19th century

The horse in agriculture

Early man was a nomad, always searching for food. He used first the wild dog and then the wild horse to help him in his hunt for food. Then man turned farmer and began to grow his own crops and raise his own cattle. The horse became even more important to him. He found that cattle strayed—just as they do to-day—and had to be rounded up. He also needed to guard his herds and flocks by day and night against wild animals, and found that this could be done more efficiently on horseback.

In the summer, rough grazing provided a plentiful supply of food for a horse, but during the winter months food was scarce. It was this scarcity of winter food that kept the British horse so small and stunted in size for so long. Then man learnt how to grow, harvest and store grass crops for use in winter. He also invented the plough and other heavy farming tools, which enabled him to put more land under cultivation. But at first the British horse was still too small to pull the heavy plough, and oxen were used instead.

The different European races who invaded Britain brought with them the larger breeds of horses, the Great Horses of Europe. The British horses interbred with these, and this, added to the better feeding methods, eventually produced the British Heavy breeds, the draught horses—chestnut Suffolk Punch and the white-legged Shires and Clydesdales. These British draught horses are the biggest of all breeds in the world: 16–18 hands and weighing not less than a ton. They replaced the oxen in agriculture.

Ploughing in the days
before the tractor

The horse in sport: Racing

Racing is a primitive instinct in man and animal. Both dislike being outstripped in speed. Horse racing must have begun from the first moment man learnt how to tame a wild horse.

Organised racing as a sport began in Arabia, where horses were kept thirsty and trained to race to the nearest water. These horses were of the southern, hot-blooded stock — the early Arabian horses.

For centuries, eastern rulers kept great breeding stables and raced their horses to test the animals' skill and stamina.

As the Arabian conquerors spread across the eastern world to the western world, they took their Arabian horses with them. The Arabian horses, because of their slimmer build, were speedier than the Great Horses of Europe, and so eventually became the favoured horses for all types of racing.

Organised racing in Britain came with the Roman occupation. Wherever they made a permanent settlement, the Romans established the hippodrome, or circus, in which organised speed contests took place. Of course the Britons were already accomplished war charioteers when Cæsar landed in 55 B.C. The chariots they drove were modelled on those in use at the time in Greece and Rome, and their horses were a mixed breed of European and oriental stock. But organised racing was a new sport to the Britons, and, in the form of flat racing, has remained ever since.

Modern flat racing

Steeplechasing

In the days when our countryside was much wilder than it is to-day, people used to hunt and ride more frequently across open country, jumping hedges, brooks, banks and fences as they went. Perhaps one day one rider said to another something like this—'Do you see that steeple over there? I'll race you to it!' Away they went, taking the most direct route, even though that meant clearing a stream, jumping several hedges, scrambling up slippery banks, and crossing fields with crops.

So probably began the first steeplechase, from one given point, across country to a second given point, jumping anything in the way. At first the races were from village to village—from steeple to steeple —but later the races were arranged in open country, starting from a given point and taking a circular route to arrive back at the same or a nearby point.

Point-to-Point races are still held in country districts, but steeplechasing itself is now organised by the National Hunt Committee and races are held on an enclosed race-track with artificial jumps and hazards of fixed heights and distances. Sometimes these artificial hazards test a horse's abilities and endurance beyond its strength, and good horses are injured and have to be destroyed.

The horses used to-day in flat racing and steeplechasing are mainly English thoroughbreds. This is a breed of horse whose ancestor was the Arabian horse, so giving a light-weight body combined with great speed.

A high jump

Polo

Polo has been played in Persia and parts of India for many centuries. In the early days it was played on any patch of open ground without any boundaries, or even up and down any village street that was wide enough. Any number of players could take part, and the rules varied from district to district. In some parts of the East it is still played in this free-for-all way.

In the 19th century some British cavalry officers, stationed in India, watched one of these games in progress and decided to try it themselves, not only as a game but also as a way of training young cavalry officers. When one regiment, the 10th Hussars, returned from India, they arranged a match with the 9th Lancers to be played on Hounslow Heath. They used a white, ivory billiard ball, and this first match was announced as 'Hockey on Horseback'.

The horses used in this first polo match were small, wiry ponies about 12½ hands high. In time, larger horses were used, as the officers of the Indian Cavalry wished to use their troop horses in the game. Most of these horses were above this low pony height.

Polo is a fast game, so the horses and ponies used must be strong, agile and intelligent. A pony is not mature or strong enough to train for polo until it is five years old, and then it takes a further year to train to the game, with another year of lesser matches before it is fit to take part in important ones. Because of its age and length of training, a good polo pony is expensive to buy.

Polo ponies in action

Show jumping

Jumping is another of the sporting activities which has been popular for many centuries. Modern show jumping is as highly organised as racing; but whereas racing is mainly for adults, show jumping can begin with the youngest member of the local Pony Club.

Every year numerous rodeos, horse or agricultural shows are held throughout the country, and at every show, horses and riders compete against one another. There are many classes, from the novice to the highly experienced jumper.

All show jumping in Britain is under the control of the British Show Jumping Association, whose members see that the jumps, their height and type are standard; that the jumping courses are varied so as to present the most adequate test to the horse and rider; that the marking is uniform and fair, and that each show as a whole is made entertaining and understandable to the public who come to watch the competitive events.

The fascinating thing about show jumping is that a rider can begin when a small child and, through the years, work up from comparatively small, local club events to county, country and international events, perhaps ultimately reaching the highest achievement of all—that of representing his or her own country at the World Olympics.

Safely over!

Haute Ecole

Haute Ecole is an advanced system of riding which educates and trains both rider and horse to the greatest heights of perfection in horsemanship.

Early in the 16th century an advanced school of horsemanship was established in Italy by Count Cesar Fiaschi. It soon became so world famous that Henry VIII and other monarchs had Masters of the Horse from this Italian school. The present-day continental Haute Ecole developed from the teachings of these early Masters and this first Italian school.

The Spanish Riding School in Vienna is now the most famous centre for Haute Ecole and riders from all parts of the world go to it to study advanced training methods. The rider in the illustration is performing an exercise called the 'Courbette'. The School was founded at Lipizza, near Trieste, by Archduke Charles. It was then known as the Spanish Court Riding School. It began with nine, white, Arabian stallions and twenty-four brood mares of the old Spanish Andalusian breed. The horses bred were then named after the place of origin—the Lipizzanas.

At first these horses were bred for royal use. The Imperial Court of Vienna preferred Lipizzaners as riding and carriage horses, and many hundreds were bred. A nobleman never used less than six horses to draw his carriage.

In the mid-18th century, a new riding school was built as part of the royal palace. This included a vast, undercover riding hall with galleries for visitors. The Spanish Riding School is now state owned.

Performing the courbette

Police horses

In 1763, the first mounted police started duty. They were called the 'Bow Street Horse Patrole', and there were only ten of them. They had to patrol the main roads leading out of London and their duty was to catch highwaymen and prevent robberies.

In addition to preventing serious crimes on the main roads, the 'Patrole' was also used to check dangerous and reckless driving by coachmen and others driving or riding horses.

At one time nearly every Police Force had a mounted division, but now only the larger forces have a section of mounted police. The car, helicopter and motor cycle have taken over the main duties of the horse. However, a motorised vehicle is no use in controlling a large crowd. A horse moving gently sideways is far more effective for pushing back a surging crowd or making a passage through a crowd, it is even more effective than any body of police on foot.

Of course, a horse used to control great crowds, or head a procession, must be thoroughly trained. All police horses are taught to obey their rider's touch; they have to learn to walk quietly, to stand still without fear when trumpets are blaring, or when people are cheering, flags waving or whistles blowing. At the training schools they are introduced to all these strange noises, and, in addition to these, they are ridden between fires and through smoke, and *must* be trained not to panic when faced with such dangers.

A mounted policeman

Royal horses

Throughout history, the rulers of countries have always had their own personal corps of foot and mounted bodyguards, Britain's Royal Sovereign is guarded by the Household Brigade, and one section of this is known as the Household Cavalry. It is made up of two regiments—the Life Guards who wear scarlet tunics, and the Royal Horse Guards in blue tunics.

The origin of the Household Cavalry goes back to the days of the war between King and Parliament in the mid-17th century. A group of loyal friends of the exiled Charles II formed themselves into a unit, and when the King returned to this country from exile in 1660 he was escorted by eighty of his own Life Guards. On regaining the throne, Charles II then formed the Royal Horse Guards, known popularly as The Blues, from other loyal cavalier units.

When the Household Cavalry are on guard duty or taking part in state occasions, they wear the full-dress uniform dating back many centuries— the colourful tunics, steel cuirasses, steel helmets with drooping horse-hair plumes (white for Life Guards, red for Horse Guards), white buckskin pantaloons and long knee-boots.

The horses are trained to stand still for long periods without moving from the spot. They also have to learn obedience to their rider's touch, so that on ceremonial occasions, such as taking part in state processions or Trooping the Colours, they can move in strict and precise formation. Like the police horses, they also have to learn to ignore sudden or long bursts of noise around them.

*A member of the
Household Cavalry*

Pony stock

In the twelfth and early thirteenth centuries, Genghis Khan became the great conqueror of many eastern countries. His father was the lord, or khan, over vast grazing lands. These lands were raided by rival chiefs and Genghis was captured. At that time he was only eleven. He escaped, and for years he was hunted by enemies. By the time he was seventeen he had gathered around him a group of young men equally bent on righting the wrongs done to them, and of conquering in turn. This was the start of the great cavalry-army Genghis Khan was to build up. All Genghis Khan's invading troops were mounted on small, stout Mongolian ponies of northern cold-blooded stock.

When in 1219 his great Mogul cavalry force, the Horde, defeated the Moslems, Genghis Khan's kingdom then stretched from Korea to the Caspian Sea. In order to receive reports from distant commanders, he had roads built with post-stations every twenty-five miles. At each station were kept forty horses, and a rest house for the despatch riders. These riders covered one hundred and fifty miles a day. In all, there were ten thousand post-stations, and between one hundred thousand and four hundred thousand horses were kept.

These post horses were as important to Genghis Khan's successful administration of his vast Empire as his cavalry horses had been in battle. Without them he could never have kept under his control all his distant commanders and the areas they governed.

The ponies of Genghis Khan

British ponies

There were ponies in Britain long before the Romans landed. These were early Celtic ponies, but no-one can be sure of their ancestry, although it is believed that the best among them came from Arabian stock, this stock being brought into Britain by eastern traders.

When the Romans came, they brought with them horses of Arab and Spanish type which mingled with the British pony breeds. Another type came from Scandinavia and mixed with the British ponies. It is this mixture of bloodstock which eventually led to the breeds of ponies we have to-day—Welsh, Exmoor, Dartmoor, New Forest, Fell, Highland, Dale and Connemara. None of these can be called pure-bred, because all are artificially improved ponies based on Celtic stock with Arab blood, and yet all now have their individual characteristics which make it possible to pick out one breed from another.

Most of these ponies live and breed in a semi-wild state on the moors, mountain-sides and in the New Forest in Hampshire. But this does not mean they are wild animals and have no owners. All belong to farmers or horse-breeders in the area, and at regular intervals the animals are rounded up for counting, branding and recording. The young ones, as shown in the illustration, are then sold at special Horse Fairs for breaking in, mainly as riding ponies.

At a pony sale

The Shetland pony

The dainty Shetland pony is the smallest of all breeds of ponies, and is the only one in Britain to remain pure-bred over many thousands of years. The Shetland's small, compact size, very hardy constitution and isolation from other pony breeds are the reasons why it has lived unchanged through the centuries. It comes from the Shetland Isles in the far north of Scotland. In times past, food was often scarce, particularly in winter, and ponies had to live on seaweed they picked up on the seashore. This rigorous way of life, plus frequent bad weather conditions, developed in these ponies a tough resistance to all hardships.

From the Shetland Isles, the use of this pony spread to all parts of northern Scotland. In early times there were no roads in the far north of Britain, only narrow, rough tracks, so carts were not used as transport. Instead, all goods were carried in panniers strung across the pony's back. A larger pony or horse would have been useless in such rough, hilly country.

The coat of the Shetland pony is specially adapted to a cold, wet climate. In winter the hair is long with an undergrowth of fur. This long hair acts as a rain-proof thatch keeping the fur next to the skin dry and warm. In summer the coat is smooth.

The average height of a Shetland is forty inches. Because of its small size it was at one time much used down coal mines to draw coal carts. Its main use now is as a riding pony for small children. Many Shetland ponies are exported to other countries where they are kept as pets or riding ponies, or to draw small carts.

A Shetland mare and foal

Donkeys

It is believed that the donkey was originally domesticated from the Somali wild ass. This slow-moving, patient animal has been man's 'beast of burden' for thousands of years. It can carry a greater load on its back than a horse, and it is sure-footed on all kinds of difficult and dangerous mountain tracks. There are records to prove that the Egyptians used the donkeys as far back as 3000 B.C., when building their great monuments.

From numerous biblical references we know that the donkey was used in many and varied ways. It did heavy farm work, turned the mechanism controlling irrigation schemes in the desert regions, and turned the millstones used to grind grain into flour. In biblical times the donkey was also used to carry rulers and men of nobility. Such a mount was a token of a peaceful journey—the horse was reserved for war and armed soldiery—that is why Jesus entered Jerusalem riding on the colt of an ass.

There are still wild asses in various parts of the world, but the wild animals are very different from the domesticated donkeys. They are high-spirited and can move with the speed of a horse. The Mongolian wild ass can travel at the rate of forty miles an hour for the first mile.

Largest of all the Asiatic wild asses is the Kiang, or Tibetan ass. This handsome animal lives on the high mountain plateaus of Tibet where the cold is intense and life very hard indeed.

The domesticated donkey

Zebras

The distinctive black-and-white stripes of the zebra are actually its protective colouring. It likes to live in lightly-forested country and in these areas its striped coat is helpful, for the stripes blend well with the shadows of branches against sunlight or moonlight.

Its main enemy is the lion, but fortunately in addition to its natural camouflage, the zebra has a keen sense of smell, excellent eyesight, and can run very fast when necessary. Zebras move about in large herds, and in some African forests herds of more than one thousand in number have been reported.

Zebras drink regularly, so a herd seldom strays more than five miles from water. The herd on its way to water is usually led by an old stallion who goes ahead to make sure that no lurking lion is also by the water hole. When he is satisfied that all is clear, he gives the signal—a low neigh—for the others to move in.

There are three kinds of zebra in the wild to-day. Grevy's zebra is the largest, and its entire head and body are finely lined. It lives in the plains and lowlands of Abyssinia, Somaliland and northern Kenya. Burchell's zebra is the common broad-striped zebra of southern and eastern Africa. The Mountain zebra is the smallest of the three, and the most attractively marked. It lives in the mountain regions of South Africa.

Perhaps the time will come when the zebra will be domesticated to the use of man, just as the horse and ass have been. But for the present it is still a wild animal, resisting all efforts to tame it.

Zebras at a water-hole

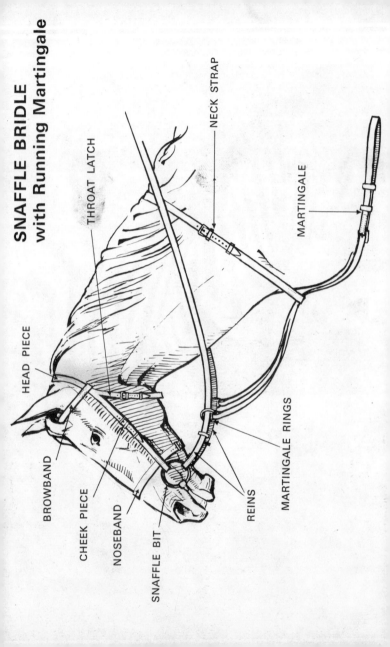

SNAFFLE BRIDLE
with Running Martingale

NECK STRAP

THROAT LATCH

MARTINGALE

HEAD PIECE

BROWBAND

CHEEK PIECE

NOSEBAND

SNAFFLE BIT

REINS

MARTINGALE RINGS